# Ella Khalifa

Illustrated by Marina Martinez

 **Mavenhill**

www.mavenhill.com

This hardcover edition 2023

Copyright © 2020 by Ella Khalifa
www.ellakhalifa.com

Mavenhill and the M book logo are registered trademarks

Cover design and book illustration by Marina Martinez
www.mapamundocomics.com

ISBN 978-1-940387-15-4

All rights reserved. No part of this book may be reproduced, scanned or distributed in any printed or electronic form without permission. Please do not participate in or encourage piracy of copyrighted materials in violation of the author's rights. Purchase only authorized editions.

**A** **is for Amore,** the Italian word for love, originating from the Latin verb *amare*. Whether it is work or fun, Italians do most things with great passion and plenty of *amore*.

**B** **is for Bravo,** a short way of saying good job all around the world. It most likely evolved from the original Italian words for *brave* or *bold*. Italian also has the feminine form (*brava*). *Bravissimo* (or *bravissima*) means super bravo!

**C is for Ciao,** an Italian word many people around the world use to say hello and goodbye. It is originally from the Venetian phrase *s-ciào vostro* or *s-ciào su* meaning *I am your slave*. In Italian, *ciao bella* (*bello* for men) means hello beautiful!

**D** **is for Dolce Vita**, or *sweet life* in English. The expression was rendered eternal by Frederico Fellini's iconic film *La Dolce Vita* featuring Marcelo Mastroianni. With its moderate climate, delicious food, rich culture and history, and natural beauty, living in Italy is arguably the quintessential *dolce vita*!

**E is for Espresso,** an Italian coffee brewed by forcing almost boiling water under pressure through finely ground coffee beans. The first espresso machine was patented by Angelo Moriondo from Turin in 1884. In many places around the world, *espresso* is called *expresso* and is considered the gold standard of good coffee.

**F is for Ferrari,** an Italian luxury sports car founded by Enzo Ferrari in 1939 out of Alfa Romeo's race division. Ferrari race cars are traditionally red. Ferraris are fun, fast and feverishly expensive!

**G is for Gelato,** Italian for ice cream and one of Italy's most celebrated desserts. It derives from *gelare*, Latin for *to freeze*. You can get gelato all over the world now, but nothing beats the original.

**H is for Hotel,** where you may be staying when you visit Italy. Like most words starting with H in Italian, it's an import (from French). Italians do not pronounce the first part of the H sound, so it's H for *otel*! *Albergo* is the actual Italian word for hotel.

**I is for Italia,** the Italian word for Italy. The color of the Italian flag may remind you of a delicious caprese salad of tomatoes, mozzarella cheese and basil. It is thought that green represents Italy's land, white for the snow-topped peaks of the Alps, and red for the blood shed during the Italian Wars of Independence and Unification.

**J is for Jacuzzi,** an iconic company that produces hot tub spas, founded by an Italian family of the same name. Jacuzzi hot tubs first appeared in 1968, based on a hydrotherapy pump the family had invented to ease the symptoms of rheumatoid arthritis. In Italian, Jacuzzi is pronounced *Yacuzzi*. That said, J is not part of the Italian alphabet.

**L is for Lasagna,** possibly one of the oldest types of pasta from the Italian city of Naples. It is made with stacked layers of flat pasta often alternated with minced meat (typically beef), tomato sauce, other vegetables like carrots and celery, and various cheeses like mozzarella and ricotta.

**M** is for **Mamma Mia,** Italian for literally *my mom*! The expression has been adopted in many parts of the world as an exclamation of awe or exacerbation. It is also the name of an iconic pop song by the Swedish band Abba, which in turn inspired films and musicals based on Abba's repertoire.

**N is for Nutella,** one of Italy's most successful food exports, invented by the Ferrero family in the 1960s. It is a creamy chocolate spread made from a secret and impossible to imitate recipe of hazelnuts, cocoa and milk. The name Nutella was created by merging the English word *nut* with the Italian positive-sounding suffix *ella*.

**O is for Opera,** a traditional art form that originated in Italy in the sixteenth and seventeenth centuries. Famous Italian operas include *Madama Butterfly*, *Turandot* and *La bohème* by Giacomo Puccini and *Aida*, *La Traviata* and *Rigoletto* by Giuseppe Verdi.

**P is for Pizza,** Italy's most famous savory dish, made from a flattened base of dough topped with tomatoes, cheese and often other ingredients. Pizza is baked at a high temperature, traditionally in a wood-fired oven. Modern pizza evolved from flatbread dishes in the city of Naples.

**Q is for Quartet,** from the Italian word *quattro* (four). It is an ensemble of four instrumental performers or singers. In classical music, one of the most common combinations of four instruments is the chamber music string quartet.

**R is for Ravioli**, a type of Italian pasta made from thin pasta dough with a meat, cheese or vegetable filling. Usually served with a sauce, ravioli first appeared in Italian cuisine in the 14th century. The word ravioli is thought to come from *riavvolgere*, Italian for *to wrap*.

**S** **is for Spaghetti,** probably the most famous of all Italian pasta. The name comes from the diminutive of *spago*, or *thin string* in Italian. Outside Italy, the most common sauce topping for spaghetti is Bolognese (*ragù alla bolognese* in Italian), a meat-based sauce typical of the city of Bologna.

**T is for Tiramisù,** an Italian dessert that literally means *pull me up*. It is made of ladyfinger biscuits dipped in coffee, layered with a whipped mixture of eggs, sugar and mascarpone cheese, flavored with cocoa and sometimes liquor. Tiramisù was first created in the 1960s in the city of Treviso.

**U is for Uno,** or the number one in Italian. It is where the informal English expression *numero uno* comes from, meaning the best or most important person or thing. It is also the name of a popular card-shedding game.

**V is for Vino**, Italian for wine. Italy is the largest producer and exporter of wine in the world. Some of the most renowned Italian wines include Barolo, Barbaresco, Brunello, Prosecco and Chianti.

**Z is for Zabaione,** an Italian dessert and sometimes a beverage made of egg yolk, sugar and a sweet wine. The dessert version is similar to a light and airy custard. Zabaione can also be a *gelato* flavor.

**K, W, X and Y** are not used in the Italian alphabet. However, some words imported from other languages use these letters like *karma*, *water* (pronounced *vater*, meaning toilet) *xenofobia* and *yogurt*.

Ella Khalifa lives in Rome with her family. Other than writing books, she loves traveling, jumping on the trampoline, playing the piano, and eating sushi. You can find out more about Ella at **www.ellakhalifa.com**

Marina Martinez is a graphic designer and illustrator based in Buenos Aires, Argentina. She draws about everyday life situations, mostly about food.
You can see more of Marina's work at **www.mapamundocomics.com**

Few countries in the world inspire love and passion in its visitors like Italy. Whether it's the delicious food and wine, timeless history, breathtaking landscapes, fast cars, or flair for fashion, Italian culture is now part of your world. Ella Khalifa, a ten-year-old living in Rome, wrote this book as proof that even if you didn't know it, you already speak Italian!

$25 • €20 • £18

**Mavenhill**

ISBN 9781940387123

www.ingramcontent.com/pod-product-compliance
Lightning Source LLC
Chambersburg PA
CBHW042316280426
43673CB00081B/397